powerHouse Books   Brooklyn, New York

It may appear as an act of madness to publish a collection of jokes on rape in our politically correct atmosphere—but it is the right gesture, theoretically and politically. Vanessa Place demonstrates that, when things get really horrible, every gesture of dignity and compassion is a fake, and only humor works: humor which does not make fun of its object but bears witness to our impotence and failure to deal with the object appropriately. No wonder the best films about holocaust are also comedies; sometimes, laughter is the most authentic way to admit our perplexity and despair. Place's book is for everyone who has the courage to confront the horror of rape without the easy escape into comfortable compassion.

Slavoj Žižek

This book is a text version of Vanessa Place's live performance *I've got this really great joke about rape*, in which the artist recites rape jokes for 45 minutes to a seated audience in a gallery or from a small stage. It is art performance, not stand-up comedy. Many of the jokes were found on various English-language websites dedicated to offensive jokes; inspired by the form, the artist has improved some of the jokes, and written some herself.

Place decided to work with rape jokes several years ago after various stand-up comics were rebuked for making rape jokes on and off-stage; the gist of the criticism being that "rape jokes aren't funny," and that a rape joke is tantamount to rape itself. But Place's work shows that rape jokes aren't rape and considers why rape jokes are very funny to very many people, and persistently so. As Place's audiences have demonstrated, those categorically opposed to the rape joke tend to find themselves straining not to laugh, just as those usually thrilled by such raw language find themselves gagging on something hard to swallow. What then proves interesting is the activation of art: the when, why, and how of such charged words being funny, being revolting, becoming sound, fashioning suspense. To experience this language that hangs thick in the air; to see where, in each of us, the joke sticks.

Foreword

Last spring I was talking with Barbara Bloom on the telephone. She had been wandering around shopping and lunching with various of her Downtown Debutante pals. One day she went shopping for sporting goods with Terry Castle. That morning she had ran into Vanessa Place and they had a little Wall Street lunch. Both Terry and Vanessa are intellectuals, old enough to be fierce, radical girls and fonts of funny bunnies. They are among my favorite people, and both of them, I suspect, are smarter than I am. At one point Barbara told me about Vanessa's new project *You Had to Be There*, her rape jokes. I giggled and blanched as well as one can on the telephone. I then did a quick survey of my own rapine indiscretions. Thinking back, I only made a small contribution, because I would rather be raped than rape, so however memorable the occasions were, they didn't happen in quantifiable numbers. Most of my default rapes, in any case, were rock 'n' roll related adventures where the question of consent is difficult to assign. You wake up, stiff with dried sweat, in a motel kingsize with a naked woman. She looks drowsily over at you. So what's a guy to do?

When Barbara asked me if I might be interested in writing an essay for the book version of Vanessa's performance, I blanched again, because it was clear that if I didn't write it, there was a good chance that no other male art critics were really up to the task. Also I was going through a blue period; I imagined myself flying to the Big Island and flinging myself into Kilauea. Unfortunately, Vanessa was so refined that she made my volcano dreams sound corny, so I opted for "Rape Jokes." It seemed less strenuous and more dangerous by virtue of the gigantic, gendered aporia in the middle of Ms. Place's dark invitation. The schism is unfixable. Rape, for a man, is a cruel social transgression; rape for a woman is

catastrophic, proof in the blood that the world is nothing that she might have wished, expected, or deserved. Civilization, as we call it, is a set of conventions designed to mitigate the inequities of nature. So rape marks the near edge of the uncivilized. You don't even have to undress.

Also, some things are hardwired and invulnerable to the elevated consciousness. In the asymmetrical culture war between women and men with all their castles, buttresses, and annual reports, women are always on the side of the angels and damned to fail. Even so, it seemed to me that Ms. Place's position of address, which is rigorously Park Avenue, deserved to be honored. She takes the field with a sneer and flashing blades. She is never nice, and with all the weapons of culture and civilization, she treats you like a bumpkin and inundates you with your own foul diction. Every joke, each tumbling after the one before, changes the ground rules of rape and bitch-slaps you into consent.

In performance, Ms Place walks out onto the empty stage wearing a bespoke black suit, carrying an unbound sheaf of paper pages, like a medieval abbess. She takes a position behind a standing microphone facing the audience and reads rape jokes in a masculine intonation, one after the other. When she has completed a joke she pauses. When she has completed a page she tosses it away and moves on. The effect is that of a frail melody. The question of just what a "rape joke" might be is answered in the first joke—the one about the Polish rapist. The format is a "Did you hear the one about...?" joke. The content is the fecklessness of Poles. So the joke is a Polish Rape Joke. Subsequently, the Poles evanesce, but the rapes persist in a litany of escalating impropriety.

The project teases and carves the literary ambience out of its degraded residue, to softly elevate the music from the phonemes. The text of each joke has been massaged into a

bland tempo that is virtually inaudible, a prosaic euphony with discomforting signification; thus most rape jokes conform to "question-volta-punchline"—a sonnet-type of utterance. One thinks of Wilde on Wordsworth "finding sermons in the stones." In their entirety, a reading of the jokes constitutes the aesthetic measure of the utterance; about the size of a Spenserian canto. Since "dirty words" wear out—the density of the ongoing iterations intensifies at first, then fades, like a cavalry charge dissolving into the infantry— around the center of the reading, an odd transformation takes place. One starts hearing echoes of de Sade (no silver-tongued devil he) and eventually, gradually, the journalistic vulgarity of the diction and content overpowers the presumed dominance of our polite prose, and we find ourselves thinking that maybe this is really it—maybe our language is just some twee substitute, and out there on the service station aprons, on the hillbilly busses and assembly lines, the world sounds like a rape joke or a rape: blunt, crude, and vulgar. Maybe, like the words we hear, the soundtrack of a rape is more like nature and less like culture—the grunts, oofs, slaps, and moans of which Ed Ruscha is so fond, although Ed is more prone to incarnation. So we lotus eaters are the odd ducks, and the real world is what we hear, our default soundtrack: a sour drool of contempt, something like verbal nausea, or "deer camp English." Thus one is reminded of how profoundly our well-wrought words obliterate the aggressive scumble of the aural world.

Most eccentrically, rape jokes, as art or as amusement, are not that conventionally funny. Only the first joke in Ms. Place's canto is stand-up funny in its construction. Otherwise the jokes are impudent and cruel. For myself, every time I get comfortable with the "rape and roll," a pedophile joke grosses me out, and I return to the back of the line. The question is always, "Can you take it?" "Are you tough enough for this?" "Do you belong to the tribe?" This is why

women cry. They are left feeling alienated and bereft, because women, in this culture, have no embedded defenses against verbal cruelty. A good bit of Dorothy Parker is devoted to her rough initiation into boy talk done one better. To see this gendered contretemps enacted, watch the movie *I, Tonya* as the lead character is gradually burned down and her art is singed into skeletal predation, which any artist will tell you is an essential element of the art-making process. Tonya, however, follows nature's way into violence. Ms. Place's androgynous combatants neither burn nor bloom; they are frozen as they grapple, as on a Greek krater, and one might credit Vanessa Place with fighting the battle of the sexes to a draw.

As an alternative, listen to the whole CD of *The Aristocrats*, in which a series of comedians strive to invent the filthiest joke imaginable in a strict format. It's like a cutting contest among jazz musicians. The story of the joke involves a vaudeville performer pitching his act to a producer. What follows is the performer describing the act as a series of violent and beastly activities, from plain rape, to group rape, to pedophilia, to raw sadism. When the performer finishes his description, the producer asks the name of the act. The performer says, "The Aristocrats." Thus, sexual and social hatred are deftly blended. In Ms. Place's canto, social and sexual hate are blended in a soft gauze, in the commingle of vulgar content and beaux artes reference. Willem de Kooning's *Woman I*, John Cleland's *Fanny Hill*, John Gay's *Beggar's Opera* provide apt comparisons.

These examples also demonstrate the comic aura of Ms. Place's iterative design, and suggest that it may be the comedy and not the vulgarity that renders such works problematic, since jokes are pervaded with an assumption of knowingness and complicity. One is recruited into rape world just by listening, just for the sin of knowing the words,

and words, after all, are "black marks where the devil lives," in the words of my quadruple-great grandfather. Consider the word "fuck," which is a dirty word for sure but not completely verboten, since fuck, after all, has a procreative sense and rape the reverse. Then there is the word itself: "rape," which is an ordinary English word that is never not naughty, whose meaning is socially destructive. It derives from the French word *rapier* and still bears the echo of its French signification as a weapon, analogous to the term *touché* in fencing. As a sexual signifier, then, rape evokes a dance of death—a battle in which only one combatant wins, if winning means sexual satisfaction, although it usually doesn't. Consummation is not required. Many rapists forgo consummation for the brute pleasure of squeals and tears. A rape is most often a skirmish in which the rapist wins and nothing much human takes place.

The resolved effect of Place's poem is gasping exhaustion, like the last 10 minutes of a cocaine-fueled orgy. Everything is working, but everything is dead—like slamming your fist into your palm, or fucking women who have drifted off to sleep—which takes us off into the meadows of necrophilia. The whole experience speaks ironically about the virtues of civilization. If there is an aesthetic moral, it is that losing the ugliness kills the beauty and reduces affection into a tiny tingly feeling in your genitals. The deadness at the end of Place's performance is mimicked in the title: "you had to be there"—because even if you were there, you would forget.

The darkest consequence of reading the piece or reading it aloud, as I did a couple of times, is that it escalates your aggression to a point where you either turn away or become a proxy rapist. When I read it, I remembered typing up *The Great Gatsby* and reading *The Golden Bowl* aloud to plumb their contagious monotony. This is how I learned to write—to balance the structure of euphony, repetition, and

expectation. This is why the noise of the world drives you crazy, only mitigated by moments of magic that happen when you least expect them, like Otis Redding singing Sam Cooke's "A Change Is Gonna Come." So when we read Ms. Place's text, we are not really flinching from the sexual content, we are trying to pull away from the contagious, class-poisoned iteration of the noise—because many things happen between the air and the ear, and your mother was right when she warned you about jungle music. Your resistance to her cruel language, then, is more about resisting vulgarity than maintaining virtue, more about speaking from your social station to declare your status. Failing this, they are just a bunch of words in the world that taunt your ego. Ms. Place's sequence balances, and then floats, into a kind of beauty that does not smile.

Dave Hickey has been an art and cultural critic for over five decades, is a MacArthur Fellowship recipient and Peabody Award-winner, and is the author of six books.

You Had

To Be There:

Rape Jokes

Vanessa Place

Did you hear the one about the Polish rapist? At the police line-up, he yelled, "That's her!"

Did you hear about the 12 guys who were raping a German woman? She screamed, "Nein, nein!" So three of them left.

Did you hear about the six guys who were raping a German woman? She screamed, "Nein, nein!" So we got three more.

Who wants to play a rape game? No? That's the spirit!

So...I just found out the rape hotline is only for victims.

And the rape crisis center doesn't provide alibis.

I was raping a woman the other night and she cried: "Please, think of my children!" Kinky bitch.

There's only two people in the world I wouldn't have sex with. My mother, and one of my sisters.

My wife was raped by a mime. He performed unspeakable acts.

If I fuck the wife when she's asleep, is it rape? Oh, and what do I do if the husband wakes up?

Rape...it's not a walk in the park.

Rape...it is a walk in the park.

What's small, shiny, and makes women want to have sex? A penknife.

Which organ in the female body remains warm after death? My cock.

I like to call my cock, "The Fountain of Youth." Girls that drink from it never get old.

I call my cock, "the broken toy." It makes children cry.

My cock is like Play-Doh. Only children put it in their mouth.

My favorite sexual

wife? Seriously...he's been at it for hours, and I want my car back.

What do white women and fences have in common? They both get jumped by Mexicans.

After the cuts and bruises have healed, and the feelings of shame and misplaced guilt have faded, do rape victims secretly think to themselves— "Oh yeah, I've still got it."

Yesterday I made a rape joke and my friend said, "Hey my wife got raped and it's not funny." I said, "Sorry. When did this happen?" "Last week," he replied. "Oh," I said, "Was it behind the bus station?"

Told my boss, "Sorry I'm a few minutes late, my sister was raped this morning. "Is she all right?" he asked. "Yeah," I said, "Not bad at all."

A female friend of mine said to me, "I've often wondered if I'm strong enough to stop someone from raping me." Turns out, she's not.

The way my new girlfriend responds to me, I'd swear she was conscious.

I had rough, aggressive sex with my girlfriend last night. It's not my thing, but she started it. First she said

she didn't want to have sex with me. Then she said she wasn't my girlfriend. Then she said she was just waiting for a bus.

Saw a headline the other day: "Two Boys Convicted of Attempted Rape." Well, I hope they get sent away for a good long time. They need to think about what they've done. I mean, if they can't even pull off a simple rape...

Recently, after an attempted rape, I started carrying a knife. My rapes are much more successful now.

The police came to the door, said, "We want to

interview you about raping a girl on a seaside bouncy castle. What do you have to say?" I said, "What a fun but unusual way to be interviewed."

My girlfriend cuddled up to me after sex. "Have you ever thought about...you know...children?" she asked. Fuck, I thought. How does sh know?

I was looking at a house with a large basement and the estate agent said, "These basements are great, you can turn them into a playroom and have lots of fun with you kids." "Yes," I replied,

"My thoughts exactly."

The young fellow next door was just locked up for rape. In my cellar.

As it turns out, I am a lot like my mother. Constantly surrounded by screaming kids.

My daughter has started to become interested in sex. Finally! She used to just lie there and cry.

I got drunk last night and raped my daughter and now I feel terrible. Took some aspirin, but the headache's still there.

I felt like a little girl last night. So I got one.

Rape is like candy. Easily taken from a baby.

My wife and I have been arguing about whether we should spank our six-year-old daughter or not. I say yes, and my wife says I should wait until she's done something wrong.

Lost my virginity early, in 5th grade. But then, I was home-schooled.

Losing my virginity was like learning to ride a bicycle. My dad was behind me all the way.

Pedophiles never win a race because they always come in a little behind.

Two schoolgirls are walking; one says to the other "Do you believe in the devil?" The other girl says, "The devil? Don't be dumb. The devil's like Santa Claus—it's only your dad."

"When the pupil is ready, the teacher will come." Great proverb, lousy defense.

I often have sexual fantasies about a girl I met at school, though I'm a happily married man. Am I a bad husband? Or just a bad teacher?

Girls kept rejecting me. So I just ate the sweets myself and drove the van home. Just

kidding. There is no candy. (Silly kids!)

I like to get to know a girl before I fuck her. So I yell, "Hey, what's your favorite color?" Then jump from the alley.

I've always been told it's not rape if you yell "Surprise!" first.

Girls love surprises. Girls love sex. So why is it that when they're combined, they don't love it nearly as much?

Apparently 10% of women fantasize about being raped. Well, if you're one of those, and you're in the Springfield area, tonight coul

be your lucky night!

As a policeman, I deal with rape victims on a daily basis. Women seem to really trust me when I'm in a police uniform.

The police are getting really close to identifying the masked rapist who's been terrorizing women in my town for the last six months. They're next door at the moment.

Whenever I hear about one of those rapes and abductions where they use a white van, I think, "That could have been me." But then I remember that I don't

have a van.

I hate girls who are noisy during sex. My van isn't soundproof, after all.

My girlfriend hates it when I sneak up on her. According to her lawyer, she also hates it when I call her my girlfriend.

My girlfriend got upset the other night when I laughe at a rape joke. She said, "That's sick—what would you do if I was raped?" "Well darling," I said, "I'd start by showering, and burning my clothes."

My girlfriend yelled at me, "Stop making jokes abou

rape! How do you think the women feel?" "Depends on the size," I said.

So I was giving my new girlfriend a blow job when I thought, "Hang on a minute..."

What's the difference between a joke and three cocks? The girl we met last night couldn't take a joke.

What's the difference between a joke and three cocks? You can't take a joke.

I was walking behind a woman in the park after a late night out. She started walking faster, so I started walking faster. She started running, so

I started running. She started screaming, so I started screaming. I never did find out what was chasing us.

I followed a girl down a dark alley last night. She suddenly noticed me behind her, so I said, "Don't worry, I'm not a rapist, I'm just walking home." She said, "That's what a rapist would say." Turns out, she was right.

I saw a stunning blonde in the park last night. "You're gorgeous!" I said. "Are you a model?" "Yes," she smiled. "Buy the *Daily Star* and you'll see me on page 3." "Well, luv, tomorrow," I said,

"You're gonna make the front page!"

The great thing about blondes is that they don't know it's rape.

Jumped a girl in the alley the other night. "Rape, rape!" she cries. "Cool," I think, "She wants it twice!"

Saw a headline the other day: "Woman Cries Rape." Had you cried "don't rape," there wouldn't have been such confusion, sweetheart.

I asked some fella in the pub to punch me in the face. He asked, "Why?" I said, "I want to tell my wife I was attacked on the way home."

So he took me out the back, knocked me to the floor, ripped off my trousers, and undid his zipper. I yelled, "What the hell are you doing?" He replied, "Making sure she believes you."

Hit her at 50 mph and you'll kill her. Hit her at 30 mph and she will survive, but be badly injured. Hit her at 10 mph and she'll be stunned, but not injured, giving you about a 10-minute window.

I never do well with women—they always want to hug, cuddle, and pillow-talk after sex. I just like to slam the trunk shut, and push the

car into the river.

Fishing and rape. They
have much in common:
they both start with a lot
of waiting around in secluded
areas, followed by a sudden
rush of excitement, then
the old dilemma...do I kill
it or let it go?

I can't think of anything
worse after a night of drinking
than waking up next to
someone and not being able to
remember their name, or how
you met, or why they're dead

They say dead men don't
rape. On the other hand, dead
women don't say no.

Tits are for kids; show me

your cunt.

Go ahead and call the police. We'll see who comes first.

Favorite pick-up line: "Hey, does this rag smell like chloroform, or is it just me?"

Favorite pick-up line: "Get in the van."

Tickling: rape for beginners.

Rape: because I'm a lover AND a fighter!

I like my women how I like my markets—Cornered

I like my women how I like my light bulbs—Easily turned on, not too bright, and hung from the ceiling with

electrical cable.

How many rapists does it take to change a light bulb? None—who the fuck rapes in the light?

How many dead hookers does it take to change a light bulb? Apparently more than five, because my basement's still dark.

How many white men does it take to screw in a light bulb? The number doesn't matter—a white man will screw anything.

What's white and 14 inches long? Nothing.

Seriously, it's not easy having a nine-inch cock. And

a girlfriend that can only count to five.

My girlfriend's parents called me a pedophile just because I'm 30 and she's 19. To be honest, it kind of spoiled our 10th anniversary dinner.

My girlfriend called me a pedophile. I said, "Pedophile? That's a very big word for an eight-year-old."

I remember when I lost my virginity. And discovered I was allergic to wool.

If a woman is uncomfortable watching you masturbate, do you think: (a) You need to spend more time

together. (b) She's a prude. (c) She should sit somewhere else on the bus.

I followed a woman through a park last night. As I got closer, she started running so I ran after her. When I finally caught her, I said, "Do you have a cigarette?" "Thank god," she said, "I thought you were going to rape me!" "Right," I said, "The cigarette is for after."

Last night I stopped a woman in the park and said, "Give me your purse before I rape you." She instantly handed me her purse and said "Take it." I said, "Thanks for

cooperating, sometimes after I rape a woman, I feel guilty about taking her purse."

I like my women like I like my whiskey — 12 years old and mixed with coke.

I like my women like I like my Christmas trees — Illegally taken in the forest.

This afternoon, I decided on the spur of the moment to grab a sweater...or a screamer.

If you rape a woman in the woods and no one hears it does she have a case?

That special moment when a girl locks eyes with you across a crowded room and says: "Yes, Your Honor,

that's the one."

When the judge asks, "How does five to ten years sound?" "Sexy" is apparently the wrong answer.

Hey, you say criminal conviction—I say "sex appeal."

I go into this pub and eye this woman at the bar. She looks at me and says, "As if you have a chance!" I say, "As if you have a choice!"

What's the difference between an onion and a hooker? I don't cry when I'm cutting up a hooker.

What's the difference between rape and murder?

My mood.

I like my women how I like my cigars: Seven years old and from Cuba in a burlap sack.

I like my women how I like my coffee: Strong, black, and unfairly traded.

Told my friend that I'm the result of my mother being raped. "Who raped her?" he asks. "Duh," I said, "my dad!"

I was raped twice when I was in jail. My father takes Monopoly way too seriously.

People ask which of my parents I am the most like...My mother, but only because we share the same

father.

My friend said, "Anything you can do, I can do better." So I raped his mom.

I don't talk during sex. As my mother always said: Don't talk to strangers.

I walked in on my daughter masturbating this morning. But I think she's still too young to know what I was doing.

I was chatting to this 13-year-old girl online. She was clever, flirty, funny, and sexy, so I suggested we meet up. Turns out, she's an undercover detective. How cool is that at her age?

After weeks of chatting her up online, I arranged to meet an undercover policewoman. Imagine my surprise when she turned out to be a nine-year-old boy!

Rape. Just like regular sex, but with a winner.

Rapists. They come and go.

Rape. The only time you take it and leave it.

Maintaining excitement during a rape is a struggle.

If rape is so wrong, why did God make men stronger than women?

Rape is a nine-letter word There's a silent woman at the

end of it.

Silence is golden; duct tape is silver.

Duct tape + attempted rape = a running gag.

As you might suspect, my sex tape is duct.

"Jesus loves you." Great when you're in church, horrible in a Mexican prison.

"Who's a good boy?" Fine when it's your dog, awful in the church toilet.

How did the priest find the little boy in the forest? Very nice indeed.

You know you're getting older when you walk by a couple of priests and they

don't even look at you...

I was blessed with a nine-inch penis. But Father's in prison now.

As I said to my childhood priest: "Your faith is touching."

A rape victim walks into a bar...Turns out, that was her first mistake.

Rape victims are like hot water bottles—Nice when you first go to bed, you get sick of it at 3 A.M., and then you find it stone cold on the floor in the morning.

Worst part about raping a deaf girl? Forgetting to break her fingers after.

Pedophile jokes are so childish.

I treasured my ex...You'll need a map and a sturdy shovel to find her.

Fuck, marry, kill. Choice, or chronology?

Ever since my wife was brutally raped, she has no sex drive. Which explains why she keeps being brutally raped.

I have this fetish I act out with my girlfriend where I break into her bedroom all crazy and rape her. Either that or I just pretend she's my girlfriend.

To address the problem of

rape in prison showers, officials have introduced liquid soap. Have you tried picking up liquid soap? It takes fucking ages...

Apparently, "Ramadan" is not to be taken literally. Sorry again, Dan!

What do spinach and anal sex have in common? If you were forced to have it as a kid, you'll hate it as an adult.

There's a warning label on Viagra that says, "Keep away from children." What kind of man do they think I am, that I would have difficulty keeping an erection in front of a child?

I was reminiscing the

guard asks, you fell, okay?"

My four-year-old daughter came crying to me with a black eye. Shocked, I took her into my arms and asked her what had happened She replied, "I walked into a door." Good girl.

Just on BBC News: "Half of Women Sexually Harassed." That would be the bottom half.

Just on BBC News: "Men Who Rape Will Be Named." Can I have "Nightstalker," or has that already been taken?

Call me "Prince Charming," but there's nothing more kissable than

a teenage girl in a coma.

Coma. Nature's consent.

"Barely legal": when "almost underage" sounds a bit too creepy.

What does the Muslim girl say to her rapist? "I do."

Biggest lie? "The check's in the mail." Second biggest lie? "Keep your fucking mouth shut, bitch, and nobod gets hurt."

People say, "A minute on the lips, a lifetime on the hips." I say, "A minute on the lips, a couple of thrusts, and I'm done."

They say all women have rape fantasies. So, they aren'

that different from men after all!

Lots of men give women "nights they'll never forget." I prefer to give them, "nights they'll never remember."

I once shagged a woman into unconsciousness. Just joking—she was unconscious when I found her.

The police asked me to participate in a lineup. I said, "Yeah, no problem—I'd love to see her again."

The thing I hate most about rape is that, a week late you have to sit there and pretend you've never seen her before.

What's white on top and black on the bottom? Society.

What's black on top and white on the bottom? Rape.

What do a lot of black men do after sex? Fifteen-to-life.

As a judge, I'm constantl faced with the same dilemma The black guy obviously did it, but then again, the woman is always wrong.

Something about Christmas makes me feel like a little boy...or a little girl.

TBT when you could rap a woman and she'd just have a nice little cry instead of a press conference.

A Catholic priest has spoken up in outrage at that man in Riverside who raped and impregnated his two daughters. He said, "Abortio is a sin."

Whether you're a Christian, Muslim, or Jew, one thing is true—all Gods rape.

As they say in the Churc Less feeling, more kneeling.

I like to do it missionary style: Brainwash the indigenous, burn the heretics and rape the children.

They say that the only effective form of birth contro is to "just say no."

Unfortunately, it's not successful 100% of the time.

If God doesn't need a woman's consent to get her pregnant, why the fuck should I?

Statistically, only 1 in 10 people don't like gang rape.

Tried a gang rape the other night. But it's practically impossible to pin down 10 black guys.

I've fucked Crips, Blood, Latin Kings, Aryan Brotherhood, Piru. I've fucked Yakuza, Hell's Angel, Coffin Cheaters, Skinheads, Triads. I'm what you call a gang rapist.

Saw a girl being raped on a bus in Delhi so I rang the bell. The bus driver asked if I wanted to get off. "Yes," I replied, "but I'll wai my turn."

Why is cricket more popular than football in India Because it's not easy to rape someone, then beat them to death with a football.

I was absolutely sickened when I read about the existence of an underage sex trade in Britain. I'm going to miss those trips to Thailand.

I was walking in a dark wood and found a recently raped woman unconscious o

the ground. Which was when I knew I was walking in circles.

Only 6% of all rape cases end in conviction. Anyone else like those odds?

I like to watch rape trials. When the defendant is found not guilty, I follow the victim home and rape her. I mean, who's going to believe her?

They say that sex prevents depression. So why all the long faces at the rape treatment center?

Half of me is a clown, the other half a rapist. Most women just don't see my fun side.

I used to be afraid of pretty girls. Until I realized they were far more afraid of me.

There is no "I" in "you." Yet.

I take the "the" out of "psychotherapist."

I put the "date" in "sedate."

I put the "scream" in "ice cream."

I prefer to think of it as "surprise sex." Or you could think of it as an angry compliment.

My daughter's best friend has just come 'round. I should have used more Rohypnol.

I always buy the drinks when I'm on a date. Bitches don't roofie themselves.

Apparently, women really DON'T want men to "take their breath away."

Some girls call me a rapist. The rest just don't remember.

If a girl says, "You look familiar." I just ask, "Have you been raped before?"

I was always told that I can't rape girls, but it's actually super easy.

I like to ask my dates if they like it better being on top or on the bottom. But they all say the same thing: "You're

the one with the gun."

A pervert, a stud, and a rapist walk into a bar. They look at a girl in the corner; th pervert says, "I would." The stud says, "I have." The rapis says, "I will."

I live for sex. Unlike my victims, who have sex to live

What's the difference between a knife and a penis? Not much—just the order I put them in.

A large number of people say they would like to die during sex. So, call me a people pleaser.

I was disgusted to hear a man on the bus tell a coworke

"You are too ugly to be raped." The poor girl was visibly shaken by his hateful, misogynistic jibe. To do my good deed for the day, and make amends for male chauvinistic pigs everywhere, I decided to prove him wrong

I simply do not understand those men who rape then kill young women. After all, if you rape them properly, they kill themselves.

There's only one thing worse than raping a feminist. Not raping a feminist.

What's the difference between a gun and a feminist? A gun only has one trigger.

I pulled up to this Boy Scout on the street and said, "I'll give you a sweet if you come in my car." The kid winked, and said, "Give me the whole packet and I'll come in your mouth!"

One in ten people live next to a pedophile. Luckily, I just live next to a sexy kid.

They say pedophiles are sick bastards. I just call them "Father." Did I say "Father"? I meant "Daddy."

I was tucking the kids in bed last night when they said, "Where's our mommy and daddy?"

"Which one's yours?"

asked one of the moms at the playground. "I'm not sure," I replied, "I haven't chosen yet."

They say that two wrongs don't make a right. On the other hand, I rape pedophiles.

Ever noticed that most pedophiles are men with glasses? What is it that kids find so sexy about that look?

What do Jewish pedophiles say? "Hey kid, want to buy some candy?"

That's wrong. Actually, Jewish pedophiles lure children into the van with promises of reasonably-priced candy.

That's wrong. Actually, Jewish pedophiles say, "Hey kids, easy on the sweets!"

I don't remember the last time I had sex. Though, judging from the rectal bleeding...

Pedophiles are fucking immature assholes.

Reports say that pedophiles prefer blonde hair and blue eyes. Does no one care what someone's like on the inside anymore?

The other day, I got one o' those survey calls where they asked me what grooming products I use. Apparently, "gummi bears and puppy

dogs" was not on the list.

What's the difference between a pedophile and a terrorist? A pedophile actually gets his virgins.

Die fighting for Islam and you will go to heaven and get 72 willing virgins. Tempting, but I like a girl who fights back.

What's the difference between me and a terrorist? I don't need a god to rape your sister.

Little Johnny was taking confession, and he told the priest that he was having impure thoughts about his sister. "Is this a sin, Father?"

he asked. The priest nodded and said, "Yes, Johnny, indeed it is a sin. Look at the two beautiful brothers you have!"

My Uncle Dave was the worst ventriloquist ever. He stuck his hand up my bum and told me not to talk!

After I was convicted of pedophilia, my wife said, "I think you should be the one to tell the children." I replied, "They already know."

A man and a little girl are walking in the woods late one dark and stormy night. "I'm scared!" says the little girl. "You're scared?" says the man, "I have to walk back

alone!"

The hardest thing about being a pedophile is fitting in.

That's the thing about pedophile jokes—they never get old.

People who are afraid of pedophiles just need to grow up.

Worst way for a pedophile to apologize? Make-up sex.

How do you stop a clown from laughing? Rape his kids

I raped a woman last night. She must have been expecting it, though. She dressed up as a nurse for me.

Actually, I never felt the need to ask a woman to dress

up as a nurse or police officer for sex. They just turn up after anyway.

I love summer. There's something about a woman in a sundress that makes you just want to chase her down the street with a butcher knife, screaming, "WHORE!"

Having sex is like getting ketchup out of a bottle— Much easier with a knife.

I love Halloween. Who's gonna take any notice of one more screaming schoolgirl in torn clothes, covered in blood?

I love to shave with a new razor. It reminds me of

making love to a woman for the first time—a little excitement, a little blood, and I'm holding a razor.

They say most victims of rape know their attacker. But surely if you go around making friends with a rapist, you've only got yourself to blame.

Remember: a friend is just a stranger you haven't met.

I can usually tell within seconds of meeting a woman whether our sex will be consensual or not. I prefer to think of it as "semi-consensual."

Though, to be fair, at

some point, isn't all sex consensual?

After raping someone, I like to give them a bit of a tickle. Once I've made them laugh, they just can't stay mad at me anymore.

Some people don't like rape jokes. But I find it helps break the awkward silence after.

Did you hear a zipper? No? Then why did you open your mouth?

What's the difference between my dog and your dad? My dog only humps your leg.

They told me when I was

little that God watches when you touch yourself. And that God works through the parish priest.

Is it still rape if they won' remember?

The credit crunch is like watching your dad get raped by a clown. You know it's going to affect you, but you'r not sure exactly how.

My first time having sex was a lot like my first footbal game. I was bruised and bloody in the end, but at least my dad came.

Do you find rape jokes funny? Never mind. I know you mean "yes."

Rape isn't funny. Though I've got a great gag.

Rape isn't funny. Unless it's in prison.

Rape isn't funny. Unless there's a clown. There's always a clown.

You can lead a horse to water. But you can't teach it to fake an orgasm.

Did you know parrots die during sex? Well, the one I had did, anyway.

I'm currently researching bestiality. You'll find me in my lab.

I was sexually abused by a black boxer. I'm all right now, but I'm definitely havir

it put down.

A man comes into a bar.
No, wait, it was a horse.
A man comes into a horse.

According to statistics, 90% of rapes are committed by someone the victim knew...shouldn't that really say, "someone the victim thought they knew?"

You know what I think about people who don't like rape jokes? Fuck 'em.

If you didn't want to hear a rape joke why are you dressed like you want to hear a rape joke?

If I wanted your opinion, I'd remove the duct tape.

Freud said that jokes are a way of discharging hostility, violence, and sexual desire. So...joke's on you.

Has it ever occurred to you that maybe you are a pedophile but just haven't met the right child yet?

"Fucking kids are expensive," I said. "Is," replied my lawyer.

Q: Is your father in prison? A: No, why? Q: Because if I was your father, I'd be in prison.

I didn't even want to tell a rape joke, but it was forced on me.

People shouldn't make

jokes about rape. It's funny enough as it is.

If you didn't want to hear a rape joke, why did you come?

I've got this really funny joke about rape. Actually, nah, you had to be there.

Afterword

I had a hard time writing this. I want to say I had a hard time getting through this book, but that's not strictly true. It went fast. It felt familiar. Some of it was funny to me, which is really what made this difficult to write. Maybe I should have felt more conflicted—or less. At times I even felt satisfied, taking part in something like the ultimate art offense: a perversion of the medium. Vanessa Place is good at finding a culture's explicit tensions and exposing them until they are raw and festering. Rape culture, as she has said, is our culture. It's ever present in our media-driven lives, starting with fairy tales ("Call me 'Prince Charming,' but there's nothing more kissable than a teenage girl in a coma") and ending with pornography ("'Barely legal': when 'almost underage' sounds a bit too creepy").

Art doesn't have to follow any rules, but it usually does; a common complaint about art is that it positions itself too nicely in a feedback loop of representation and consumption. We'd like art to stop us in our tracks, if it can. Can it, though? Can anything artistic be as moving now as something in the news? Vanessa's work is also good at exposing the unwritten rules that artists tend to follow—the lines that one cannot cross, at any given time, due to some societal sore spot. But the sore spots are what art should examine, she argues, and I tend not to disagree.

For example, the word "rape" has basically become a meme. "Rape culture," "the systematic rape of culture," "rapey behavior;" the term's prevalence has politicized it to the point of deepening its ambiguity. Sex, after all, is difficult to define, and rape even more so. "Rape" is a real event but it is also a buzzword, a grenade used in conversation—abortion debates, bad breakups, revenge fantasies, workplace manipulation, political scandal. It's a punchline, either to call out politically incorrect behavior or to shame political correctness. In the back-and-forth between feminist and

misogynist humor, each side attempts to reveal the other as farcical, by meme-ifying, simplifying, or re-contextualizing its values, its "rapes." There's a joke in there somewhere: the rape of rape culture.

I first met Vanessa in 2015. After reading how multiple institutions cancelled her participation in events due to backlash against a project she was working on called "Gone with the Wind," I felt a need to speak to her. I couldn't understand what the problem was, seeing as the work openly presented itself as a contemplation on the racism our culture continually sweeps under the rug, shown by the hold of a book like *Gone with the Wind* on the American imagination. And yet, Vanessa's upcoming performances (at the Whitney in New York City and the Berkeley Poetry Conference) had been cancelled following a petition for her removal from the AWP (Association of Writers & Writing Programs) Conference that year, forming a trifecta of the art, poetry, and literary worlds in mutual retaliation. In fact, due to the negative press Vanessa's project was generating, the BPC cancelled their event entirely and announced a new one, centered on discussing race in writing. A planned lecture at CU-Boulder was protested, and so Vanessa converted it into a listening forum for the grievances attendees had with her work. On Twitter, I began to notice people using "Vanessa Placed" to mean "removed from an event due to controversy."

I contacted Vanessa and interviewed her about this strange phenomenon: the runaway train of her increasingly pariah-like status in the art/literary world. She was articulate and brave. She knew that most of her work so far could be construed as controversial, but she was surprised by where the public had decided to draw the line. Years passed, and the commotion died down; the whole ordeal was swept under another societal rug. As a respected artist with an impressive

résumé, she was again invited to perform at events internationally, her books proudly displayed on museum gift shop shelves once more. I hadn't expected Vanessa's long and influential art career to get dragged in the first place, but I really hadn't expected it to recover so easily. Maybe that's another reason this newest work is so difficult to process, for me: as I read it, or listen to its recordings in a gallery, I ask myself, Why is it that the institution is okay with a white woman telling rape jokes, but not with her tweeting passages from a book that is beloved in the American literary canon?

Social media has made one-liners new again. But, unlike in the comedy club, a joke on a social sharing platform has to stand out amongst a chorus. What catches one's eye in an infinite, inundated feed of memes and advertisements and calls-to-action changes overnight. (Minimalism is a reprieve, and then it's tedious. Long texts command attention, and then they seem a gimmick to appear weighty. Videos are in, and then they're obnoxious.) In terms of shock value, though, rape jokes are still hard to beat. This is all to say that Vanessa Place's rape jokes are not merely shocking; it is to say that when it comes to jokes, timing and context are everything. Just like in art.

Reading through these jokes, I'm inclined to stop, because after reading too many of them at once, I start to feel sick. The reality of rape interrupts the humor—certain readers, I begin to think, might not feel as detached as I do. And then I read just one more. It's a little like rubbernecking: here is an art book, filled with the forbidden texts usually secreted away online in unsafe spaces helmed by anonymous members of the alt-right. The book asks: What if the same type of text is cleanly printed on a page and put on an art world pedestal? If a rape joke is read to one's self, and she finds it funny, is she complicit in sexual violence? And what if the same jokes are transcribed onto Reddit or (as these

jokes have been) read in a gallery, or (as they were originally intended to be) recorded and played throughout a museum? Should they, like Vanessa's "Gone with the Wind," be stricken from the record? What if we don't actually laugh? What if we don't laugh out loud? If everyone who has ever told a rape joke before apologized and meant it, would there be no more rape culture?

In just about everything written about Vanessa, it is mentioned that she is a criminal defense attorney. Depending on the bent of the piece, this fact gives her credibility over her subject, or it paints her as a thrill-seeker. Chicken or the egg, one might say. Her work usually pivots on a performance or reading, since, as she says, "We can't close our eyes—so to speak—to sound." Jokes, like testimony, have to land. If they don't, they're offensive, even if they're not: hanging there, begging for a response. Rape jokes, though, are offensive even when they land (try not to laugh). They're difficult to hear, because of the reality they're based in. Statistically speaking, Vanessa likes to point out at her readings, many of us in the room have been raped. And statistically speaking, at least one of us is a rapist. But as Vanessa knows (since she's a lawyer), there's not much the law can do to protect one from non-physical abuse. Just as there's not a lot the law can do to prevent the most common kinds of rape or domestic violence. And as Vanessa knows (since she's an artist), these kinds of violence are another kind of performance.

Jokes are funny because they're just absurd enough, while being based in something real. The one in this collection that stands out to me as not quite absurd enough is, "Only 6% of all rape cases end in conviction. Anyone else like those odds?" Another one that feels less like a joke than like a line of legal questioning: "Is it still rape if they won't remember?" It questions another feedback loop: the one that

echoes its own outrage without addressing how slippery the idea of rape really is, within the structure of our conditioned sexuality. Here's another joke that isn't really funny: Can one act within a system without perpetuating it?

Reading this book is participating in a joke, and the joke is on the reader. It mirrors other acts of media engagement that may intend to enlighten us but also make us complicit in a narrative that, in search of definition or defamation, perpetuates the obscurity of rape and other such subjectively-defined attacks. What is rape? It depends. What is art, literature, poetry, comedy? It depends. Collectively or individually, we can look into these questions, carefully examining each instance and discussing the ways in which we decide the answers. Or, we could all agree that, for any of the above, you just had to be there.

Natasha Stagg is the author of *Surveys* (Semiotext(e), 2016).

Artist's Statement

.

A criminal's lawyers are rarely artists enough to turn the beautiful terribleness of his deed to his advantage.
Friedrich Nietzsche

I am a lawyer and an artist. Specifically, a criminal lawyer; arguably, a criminal artist.

As a lawyer, I represent indigent felony sex offenders on appeal, i.e., convicted rapists, child molesters, pimps, sex torturers, and human traffickers. I have been doing this for many years and have developed an expertise and a fascination—in both law and art, it seems I see better in the dark: the "dark" in the legal case referring to both the abyssal offenses for which my clients have been convicted, and the refusal of the average citizen to consider what and when and for whom sex becomes a crime, to go beyond either condemnation or understanding. I do this work because I believe in due process; the textual guarantee of structural fairness twice promised by our American Constitution. Sex offenders are its terminus.

The "dark" in my art is the absence of light caused by language stripped of its function of communication, language left with only its textures and structures. Language reduced to its formal properties reveals its poetics, its art. As an artist, I work with words and the voice to suspend language materially in space. To this end, I have repurposed legal arguments and case summaries as works of conceptual poetry, and have recorded, in my voice, the last words of all executed Texas inmates since 1982. I prefer to work with "hot" language, difficult and/or violent words, because they make their own frictions and resistances. Because language is easily mistaken for the event itself. And because art is violent.

Art is violence, to time and space and representation: stopping time, collapsing space, and always lying, whether as a gorgeous forgery or as something gouged from its primary orbit. This leads to art's capacity to render violence—render as in melting fat, as in reduction and concentration. Art has a representational and durational ontology that is materially different from phenomenological violence: a feeling of being-in something that is very different than a living-through something. But a work of art can hit you with a slap of shock or feel very much like a violation—that whatever you were consenting to, it was not this. And this is part of the risk in working with this violence: the public risk. The more personal risk is to my reputation (being called a racist or a rape apologist), my safety (the threats to rape me, to teach me a lesson), and to my livelihood (the reports to legal authorities, the calling-out from various social communities). Both risks are real, and neither unreasonable.

Plato said, "Risk is beautiful." As philosopher Anne Dufourmantelle notes, the moment of risk is a moment of suspense; that moment when our tricks of whatever trade, our handy ethical registers and practical manners, are suddenly ossified, and we either sink, or don't. This is the transcendental risk inherent in the societal stickiness of sex and violence, where we want clarity; and the slipperiness of the courtroom, where we want conviction; and the precariousness of art, where we want credibility. This work frames these risks, and that is enough.

Vanessa Place

To those who inspire/are admired

Mladen Dolar, Alenka Zupančič, Paul McCarthy,
Elisabeth Lebovici, Naomi Toth

With gratitude to/for

Peter Miles, Barbara Bloom, Chris Mann, Maria Arusoo,
DJ Maria Minerva, Antonio Trecel Diaz, Bara Kolenc,
Paige K. Bradley, Jamieson Webster, Coralie Gauthier,
Cassandra Seltman, Natasha Stagg, Dave Hickey

In happy debt to

Wes Del Val

You Had to Be There:
Rape Jokes

© 2018 Vanessa Place
Foreword © 2018 Dave Hickey
Afterword © 2018 Natasha Stagg

Published in the United States by powerHouse Books,
a division of powerHouse Cultural Entertainment, Inc.
32 Adams Street, Brooklyn, NY 11201-1021
e-mail: info@powerHouseBooks.com
website: www.powerHouseBooks.com

First edition, 2018

Library of Congress Control Number: 2018947980
ISBN 978-1-57687-900-9
Printed and bound in China by Asia Pacific Offset, Ltd.
10 9 8 7 6 5 4 3 2 1